AF335706

# OF SHOES AND SHIPS AND SEALING WAX, CABBAGES AND KINGS, AND ASPIRIN AS NEEDED

# OF SHOES AND SHIPS AND SEALING WAX, CABBAGES AND KINGS, AND ASPIRIN AS NEEDED

A Potpourri of Prose, Paintings, and Verse

**George Conklin**

**VANTAGE PRESS**
New York

To Liza, Jared, Megan, and Aiden and their many friends

# Contents

# Preface

As in our previous books, we try here to bridge the gap between the real and everyday world and that of the unusual and imaginary. Our friends in the animal world can give us clues to possible futures.

# Prologue

Reach out ever higher on the cresting wave,
Reach out toward ever broader horizons.
Reach out toward a future of wondrous new hopes and
    aspirations,
As a poet has said: "Or what is a heaven for?"

# OF SHOES AND SHIPS AND
# SEALING WAX, CABBAGES AND
# KINGS, AND ASPIRIN
# AS NEEDED

# *A Tale of Two Sloths*

We watched it as it tried to cross the road, fearful it might be hit by a car, for it moved so slow, so slow. Did it know where it was going, or how it would ever get there? Poor sloth. Its future seemed so totally uncertain. It could not possibly know the terrible danger it was in.

Then we saw a second sloth on the other side of the road. Was it his friend? Or did it even know it? There was no way of knowing. But the big question: Was there any way to keep the first sloth from crossing the road with the very excellent chance of its getting killed?

So slow, so slow, so slow. It moved apace. Persistence, the epitome of persistence, yet so slow!

We watched then till the first sloth made it across the road. Praises be! Now what would happen? Could they possibly find each other? We kept our fingers crossed. Cars stopped because we stopped them and waited, waited, waited. So slow, so slow. At last we saw the two sloths were finding each other and they moved off into the woods ever so slowly. What a wonder of success. They found each other. Praises be, Praises be!

# Monkey Tree

Who said we were arboreal? Not now, of course,
but once, a good time ago. Once we were way up there
in the tops of the trees, swinging by our tails.
It may well have been a way to show our superiority.
But in any event we had found great pleasure in it,
real pleasure, more pleasure than anyone had ever
    imagined.
We could do just what we wanted. There was no one to
tell us we couldn't do this or that. There was no one to
    attack us, only a few tree branches to call our own.
Way up there above the perpetual fray.
What a life, way up there in the trees!
No wars to fight, no wars! What a life!
Why, oh why, oh why, oh, did we ever leave the trees, oh?
And start these endless wars, oh!
Why, oh why, oh why, oh?

## *Birds of a Feather*

Now look at my color. Why can't you see
how totally different you are from me?
I'm red and green, you're mottled gray,
and only a grubby shade at that.
We love color, glittering and bright,
while you only show up in black and white.
No, we're not prejudiced, heaven forbid!
Come one and come all with this simple warning:
No strange foreign birds can be allowed in our flock!

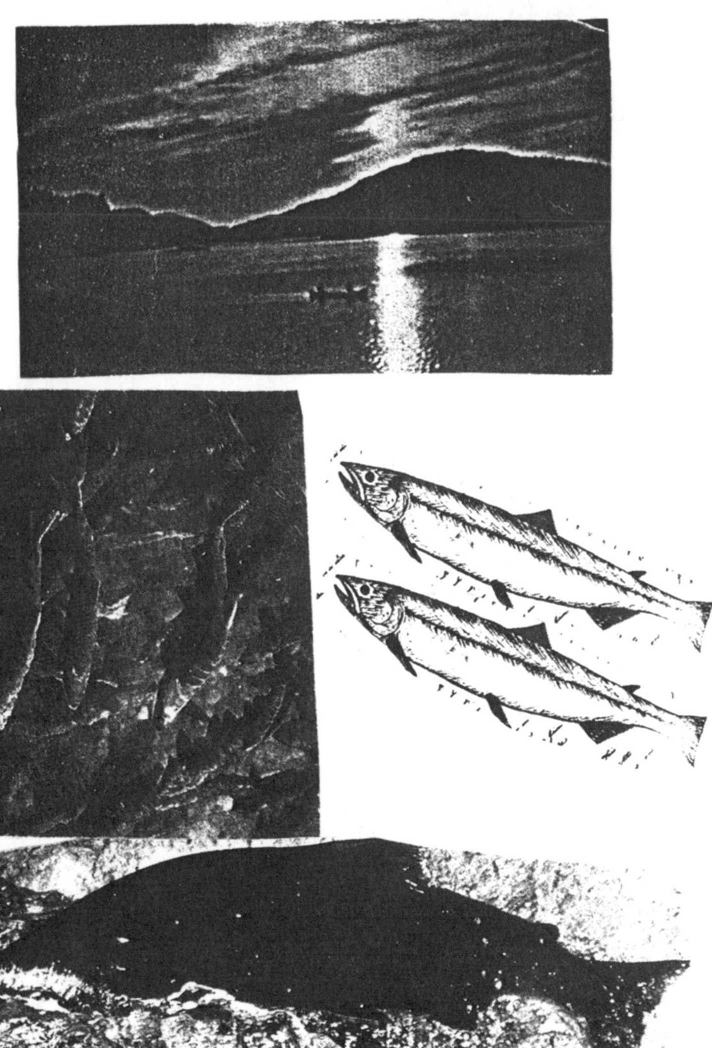

## *Fish in the Sea*

How many, many, many fish there are in the sea?
Gaudy, flamboyant, speckled and bright,
an endless variety to meet every wish
of always bigger and bigger fish.
Charles Darwin's ideas have met wide acclaim
and most especially his theory of evolution.
Races are so easy to start, it seems,
but so far as slowing the process down,
he leaves us without any kind of solution.
Everyone speaks so blithely of birth controls,
ignoring the most obvious facts (though possibly
less palatable), such as "for whom the bell tolls."

# *Round Table*

Wait there, good friend, and I'll bring you up a drink.
It's the hour, of course, the cocktail hour.
And there's plenty of room, in the front and back,
And round and round. Room for an endless number
Of good friends—amigos, muchos amigos and amigas.
No end to the number clustering round the table.
But who started it? Who knows—*quien sabe?*
Someone started it and then a second joined in,
And once there are two, there's no end to it.
They come and come from all directions.
No end to the cocktail hour, no end to the round table—
To the round, round, round table!

# **A Ballad of El Diablo**
(or The Wreck of a Wayward Brigantine)

A prouder ship you'll never know,
They called her *El Diablo*,
    the name of a famous fighting bull.

From London Bridge to Timbuctu,
She sailed the seas with a bully crew
    *El Diablo* the Incomparable.

*El Diablo* weighed anchor, her sails unfurled,
Her sights all set to circle the world;
    her coffers were always full.

A great crowd gathered on the quay
To hail *El Diablo* out to sea
    from the ancient port of Hull.

Her crew, meanwhile, could hardly wait
To pass the jug and celebrate
    *El Diablo* the Invincible.

The first night out they spiked the crock,
A swig with every roll and rock,
    the booze was plentiful.

That night *El Diablo* came to grief,
Crashing like thunder on a reef,
    with a huge hole in her hull.

"Abandon ship," the captain shouted,
And out of their bunks the boys were routed.
    "Man the lifeboats; pull, lads, pull!"

But from far inside came a tap-tap-tapping
The noise perchance of halliards flapping
    or the slap of a wayward boom.

*El Diablo* rests now on her side
Her beam awash to the rising tide
    her bowsprit gone, her hatches wide.

But still from inside came that tap-tap-tapping
Is that the sound of bowlines scraping,
    or frantic fingers scratching against the hull?

Would nary a sailor wait or wonder?
Would none give pause to pray or ponder?
    they manned their oars to strike out yonder
    as *El Diablo* went down with a pull,
    *El Diablo* the powerful!

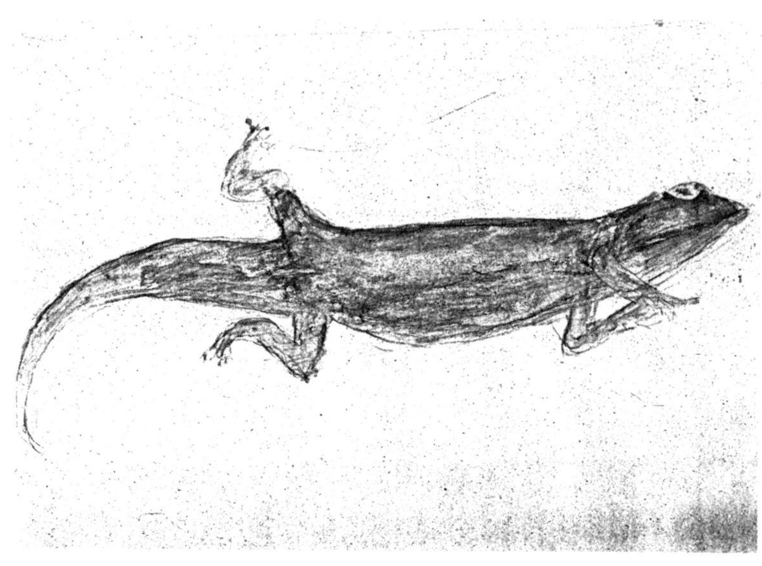

## My Gray-Green Dragon

A gray-green dragon slithers through my sleep;
    at every turn I meet his grisly grin.
I've challenged him to leave with no success,
    so he puts up with me and I with him.

We've reached a kind of understanding truce,
    each night he lights a sign: NO VACANCY,
but when day comes and my green dragon sleeps,
    we both are free—unless he dreams of me.

# An Old Buccaneer

There was now an old buccaneer.
He wore both a scowl and a sneer.
    His right buccinator was scarred with a crater
And his left held a pearl like a tear.

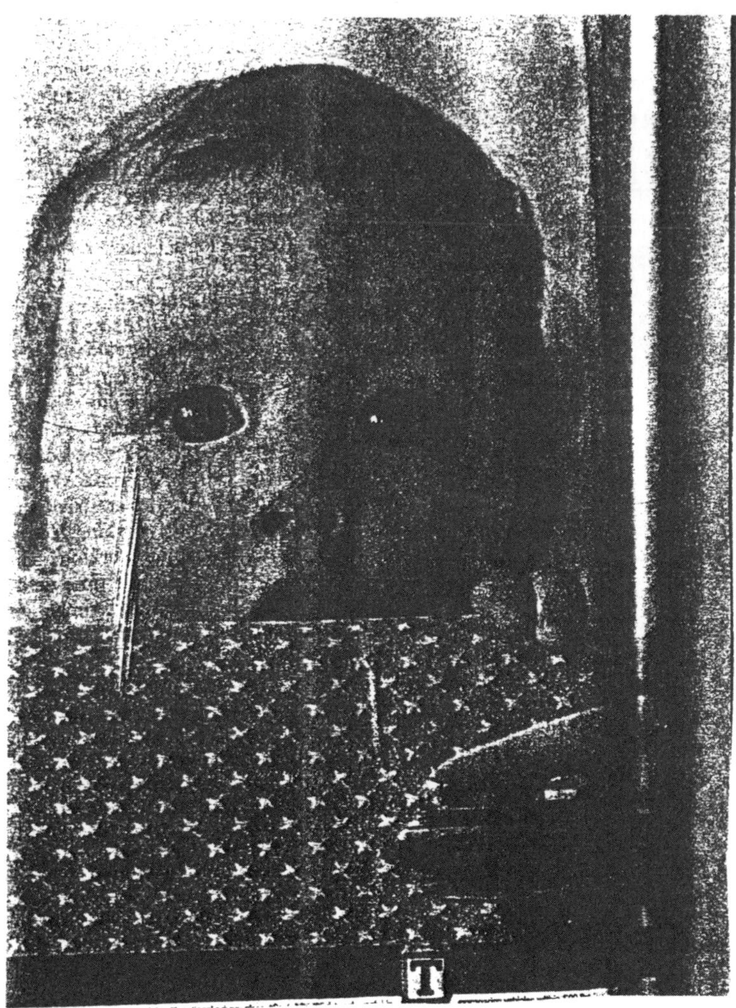

## *To Liza*

Within the simple compass of a sphere,
to live, to breathe, to wake and to see
a moving world of form and fantasy,
as out of darkness my own cry I hear!
Across the pantomime of night and day
a million shapes and figures pass in view,
a horoscope that holds so scant a clue
of how or why or where to find the way.
To grasp at every wish and try to hold
with anxious fingers what might be my own,
to learn the truth Time has so deftly sown:
In every moment's worth is more than gold.
Through summer's days and winter's nights to prove
my love for thee, that me you'll surely love!

### ***Earthbound No More***
(On the Occasion of the First Moon Landing)

Earthbound we were, earthbound no more!
So free at last that distant worlds shall envy us,
Give honor to us, honor the great minds our science bore
Earthbound, airbound no more,
Through endless eons we shall firm our grasp
And reach for the ultimate in our every thought and
    deed!

## *Far We Have Traveled*

Far we have traveled both in time and space,
And many marvelous people we have known,
And many marvelous circumstances have come our way,
Which only a master artist might fairly demonstrate;
And yet such artists are few indeed.
How often does a Mozart or Shakespeare grace the
    scene?
Once in a millennium perchance, though the world
Is flooded with a surfeit of lesser hopefuls.
We can but thank our stars for what we've known and
    seen,
For the beauty of each morning and the morning star,
Circling the sun and casting a brilliant light
Across the heavenly way, a symbol of the Lord
In all His infinite glory.

## Most Friendly Feline

Have you ever heard a cat's purr, rich and deep,
when she curls up beside you and you're going to sleep?
Whenever you hear the purr of a cat
you can always tell what she's driving at.

# *Zanzibar*

My great-great-uncle shipped to sea
    and landed in Zanzibar,
but I can't think for the life of me
    just why he went so far.

For Zanzibar was a sleazy place
    well-known for its rogues and knaves
and crooks of every caste and race
    who mostly dealt in slaves.

I think poor Uncle, bless his heart,
    had never meant to do
any such thing in Zanzibar
    as bartering a slave or two.

## *Excelsior*

Up through the eons of ooze and slime
amoebas and mollusks and thingumajigs
have slithered and shivered and quivered to climb
to the level of parrots and poodles and pigs.

Ah, had that fine level but been the conclusion!
But a new race of man, with a yen for the tomb,
like the once-dandy dodo would shun evolution
and in mammoth confusion play games with THE
    BOMB!

# *King Tut*
(November 24, 1922)

Oh King!
In all your glory there you lie,
three thousand years or more gone by
since you did proudly live and die,
    like yesterday.

Your treasures in the gloomy light,
of burnished gold and malachite,
three thousand years ago not as bright
    as yesterday.

And when did light look in your door
to see what had been seen before
three thousand years ago or more?
    Just yesterday!

## *Blubberish*

The gloshes glabble glibly
    through the glossy, glimey gloom,
and the treeterong has blunted
    on his flabbish blanderoon.

The reevers grubble ganders
    and the gart has clulled his gowl,
the bratted groon has sparted frume
    and flunted through the frowl.

In Shanteroon the film gaboon
    is shintering shone the gloval,
as shippers sheet the trovers meet
    carodeling as they blobble.

In zilling ilches flabbish bilches
    oom and abble ulb,
as through the swale the shaggertail
    beblaggers blubbers blulb.

# Sur la Plage

Oh Joy, among the shells and crabs—
   so out of place,
   a fall from grace!

   What use to clean
   so neat a scene?

   Just look at the trouble
   from one plastic bubble!

    If he could speak—
     this crabby critter—
    first thing he'd say
     is: "Stop the litter!"

Oh Joy, among the shells and crabs,
go back to your shelf and homey confabs.

## *Two Sisters*

You stay up and I'll stay down,
And we'll make a happy pair.
There's a world above and a world below,
And we each will have her share.
Of course, there are times when you visit me,
And times when I visit you,
But wherever each of us goes we may be sure
In our thoughts at least,
Neither of us will be far from the other.
You stay up and I'll stay down—
Perhaps most of all the things that bind us together
Is the remembrance of things past,
The remembrance of family affiliations and their
    continuing
And continuous assurance of mutual love.

# Tall Ships

Tall ships, tall sailing ships,
the weathered yardarms tell
of sailors reefing sails
and grasping spars.
Steel-hard they know
the clang of bells,
the tenor of a shift in wind,
and an augury of stars.

Sleep cannot still the low bass roar
of breakers at the bow. . . .
No man who has not shipped to sea can know
the eerie pity of the petrel's cry
or the sea gull's mournful call.

# *Jackie, Our Dark-Haired Water Spaniel*

When I was eight years old, my very best friend was Jackie, our water spaniel. He was so unbelievable, he was so full of life. There was absolutely no stopping him. He wanted to play every minute; he was constantly on the go. He simply ran and ran and he took to chasing every car that came along, in either our front yard or backyard. Of course we adored Jackie, my two brothers and me, and he in turn was our constant companion. In those days there was much less traffic on the roads than now, especially in the suburban area where we lived, so there was not much chance of Jackie getting hit. Yet it was Jackie's running that finally did him in. He died of a heart attack, or so the vet told us. But how were we to know? This was our first experience with death. No one had warned us of such an eventuality, and what did death mean to us anyway? We had no conception of what a world without our Jackie would be.

In any event, my father's worker was told to dig a hole and bury Jackie in it. But no, no, no, all too fast. The worker had not let Dad know when it was ready, so the worker was told to dig Jackie up again, so a proper burial could be performed, I suppose, whatever that meant. By that time it was far too much for me to take in. All I could think of was how full of life our Jackie had been. Why, yes, why couldn't it have been left at that?

# Appendix: Special Note Regarding the Sloth

Gerald Durrell wrote the following about one of his favorite animals, the two-toed sloth: "They really are enchanting creatures, their small heads, their shaggy bodies, their slightly protuberant golden eyes, and their mouths set in a perpetual dreamy, benevolent smile. Slow and gentle, they will suffer you to hang them wherever you like. . . . They are so beautifully adapted for their strange, topsy-turvy life in the tree-tops and, because they spend most of their lives upside-down, and because their diet is highly indigestible leaves, their internal organs are unlike those of any other mammal. Their whole metabolism is as slow as their movements. . . . They may go a whole week without urinating, for example."